MW01101964

RETURN TO EARTH

Some people are a little telepathic, just a little. They know what another person, perhaps a brother or a sister, is thinking. And if you know someone really well, you sometimes know what they will say before they say it.

But what is it like to be *really* telepathic? To know *everything* that other people are thinking and feeling, to know the thoughts that are hidden in their minds – every minute, every hour, day after day, like a radio that you cannot turn off. And will you like what you hear? People can think terrible things, which they never speak out loud.

Who can say what changes the future will bring? Perhaps one day, like Harl in this story, we will travel through time and space to a distant planet – and return to Earth after many long years away. Perhaps, like Ellen, we won't be interested in space travel, because we are going to change life on Earth – to do something very new, very exciting, very different . . .

Something that will change the human mind for ever . . .

OXFORD BOOKWORMS LIBRARY
Fantasy & Horror

Return to Earth

Stage 2 (700 headwords)

Series Editor: Jennifer Bassett
Founder Editor: Tricia Hedge
Activities Editors: Jennifer Bassett and Alison Baxter

JOHN CHRISTOPHER

Return to Earth

Retold by
Susan Binder

OXFORD UNIVERSITY PRESS

OXFORD

UNIVERSITY PRESS

Great Clarendon Street, Oxford OX2 6DP

Oxford University Press is a department of the University of Oxford.
It furthers the University's objective of excellence in research, scholarship,
and education by publishing worldwide in

Oxford New York

Auckland Bangkok Buenos Aires Cape Town Chennai
Dar es Salaam Delhi Hong Kong Istanbul Karachi Kolkata
Kuala Lumpur Madrid Melbourne Mexico City Mumbai
Nairobi São Paulo Shanghai Taipei Tokyo Toronto

OXFORD and OXFORD ENGLISH are registered trade marks of
Oxford University Press in the UK and in certain other countries

Original edition © John Christopher 1954
First published as 'The New Wine' in
The Twenty-Second Century, Grayson & Grayson 1954
This simplified edition © Oxford University Press 2000

The moral rights of the author have been asserted

Database right Oxford University Press (maker)

First published in Oxford Bookworms 1995
6 8 10 12 14 13 11 9 7 5

No unauthorized photocopying

All rights reserved. No part of this publication may be reproduced,
stored in a retrieval system, or transmitted, in any form or by any means,
without the prior permission in writing of Oxford University Press,
or as expressly permitted by law, or under terms agreed with the appropriate
reprographics rights organization. Enquiries concerning reproduction
outside the scope of the above should be sent to the ELT Rights Department,
Oxford University Press, at the address above

You must not circulate this book in any other binding or cover
and you must impose this same condition on any acquirer

Any websites referred to in this publication are in the public domain and
their addresses are provided by Oxford University Press for information only.
Oxford University Press disclaims any responsibility for the content

ISBN 0 19 422983 1

Printed in Spain by Unigraf S.L.

Illustrated by: Gary Bines

CONTENTS

Chapter 1

Earth 2029: A walk in the park

The leaves hurried across the park in a dance of brown and gold and red. Ellen turned her head to watch them for a minute. It was the end of October. She and Harl were walking through the trees in the last of the daylight.

'I like this time of year best,' Ellen said.

Harl watched her. She didn't look at him, and he knew what she was thinking.

'I decided to go a long time ago,' he said. 'I know there'll be no autumn leaves, no spring sunshine, and I know for how long.'

'Eight years,' Ellen said slowly. 'Eight years without summer or winter, without real days or nights. Eight years of the same food, the same life, day after day, with the same people in a little space ship fifty metres long.'

'Fifty-five,' said Harl.

'Fifty-five, then,' Ellen said angrily.

They came to the top of a small hill. Ellen stopped and looked around her. Harl stopped too, and smelled the autumn leaves and the soft warm wind. For a second he began to think that he was making a mistake – could he really leave all this behind?

Harl smelled the autumn leaves and the soft warm wind.

Ellen said: 'And it's all so unnecessary – you're going for nothing.'

Harl shook his head. He felt sure of himself again now. 'No. You're wrong. This journey is important, really important.'

'More important than me?' Ellen said softly.

She moved near him, and he took her in his arms.

'You're a good scientist,' he said. 'We need people like you. I can still get you a place on the space ship – if you want to come.'

'I'm afraid, Harl. Not of the danger, but I'm afraid of the long years of living in a small space ship. I can't do that. I need to see trees and flowers, feel the wind on my face. That year in New York nearly killed me, but cities do have some trees and parks. And there's another thing. I don't want to wait years to have children.'

Harl moved away from her.

'There you are,' he said. 'We both want different things, and neither of us will change.' He laughed. 'When I get back, I'll say hello to your great-great-granddaughter. Perhaps I'll marry her.'

Ellen shook her head. It was getting dark now, and he could not see her face easily.

'Will the time really be so different when you return?' she said. 'Are you sure about that? I can't understand how that can be true.'

3

'It's difficult to explain in a few words,' Harl said. 'But yes, we are sure. For us, our journey through space will take eight years, but for the people on this world, it will be a hundred years. So we leave Earth in the year 2029 and

'Our journey through space will take eight years.'

return in 2129 – but we ourselves will only be eight years older.'

'And all your family and friends will be dead.'

'There will be other people,' Harl said. He tried to laugh, but his voice did not sound happy. 'Like your great-great-granddaughter, for example. If I marry her, we will call our oldest daughter Ellen.'

'There will be no wives for you in the world of 2129,' Ellen said quietly.

Harl turned to look at her. 'You really mean that, don't you? Why not?'

'Because the world will be a very different place then,' she answered. 'Perhaps you'll be a hero of space travel when you return, but no one will want to live with you. It just won't be possible. To the people of 2129, you will be stranger than a wild animal in a zoo.'

'Why?' asked Harl.

'Because,' Ellen said slowly, 'you won't be a telepath.'

Chapter 2

Project X

Now Harl understood. 'Ah, you're talking about Project X. Is it going well, then?'

'We're building the generators.'

He looked at her in surprise. 'You've kept very quiet about that. Were you afraid that I would talk about it to the wrong people?'

She smiled. 'You were only interested in the plans for your space journey, and you've always laughed about my work. To you, it's just something funny – not like a dangerous journey through space to Procyon and back.'

'Yes, that's true,' said Harl. 'I thought that my project with the *Astronaut* was really important. Your Project X was strange and, well, not very serious.'

'And you're not the only person who thinks like that,' said Ellen. 'Everybody's interested in the *Astronaut* and your space journey, and so you feel important – you're already famous. But Project X is going to change our world, to make a world of telepaths. And that will be a bigger change than has ever happened before.'

He said quietly: 'Tell me about it now.'

'Oh, I see!' She laughed angrily. 'You can't explain the science of time and space to me in a few words, because it's so difficult. But you think that you can understand *my* science in just one quick lesson.'

He took her arm. 'Don't be angry. We haven't much time. Can you really begin to change some children into telepaths?'

'No. It's bigger than that; much bigger. We're going to change everybody in the world all at the same time. That will stop the new people from fighting the old – because the new telepaths will be the children of the old non-telepaths; all the children.'

She began to walk faster, and Harl had to hurry to stay by her side.

'It's Drewitt's work,' she went on. 'The other scientists in the group helped, of course, but it was Drewitt who did all the important things. He learnt that the unborn child is telepathic – it can see pictures of what its mother is thinking and feeling. Drewitt knows more about the unborn child than anyone has ever known.'

The wind was colder now. It was coming from the east, and night was falling fast.

'I never heard about that,' Harl said.

Ellen laughed, a little angrily. 'Of course not. It's only space travel that gets into the newspapers. Drewitt is a very clever scientist, but most people aren't interested in his work. Well, one day he was lucky. Usually, when a child is born, it stops being telepathic. Drewitt wanted to change that. He did a lot of experiments with monkeys, and used radiation on their unborn babies. Some very strange monkeys were born, but there were also two who were telepathic. There was no question about it. One knew what the other was thinking and feeling.'

'Drewitt did a lot of experiments with monkeys.'

Harl was listening very carefully. 'Monkeys,' he said. 'They are one thing. People are another.'

'Do you think that Drewitt didn't know that? One of the scientists in his group was a man called Whittaker . . .'

'Arthur Whittaker? I was at school with him.'

'Yes. Well, his wife also worked with the group, and she wanted to try . . .'

'You don't mean . . .?' Harl shook his head in surprise. 'Surely not!'

Ellen turned round to look at him, but in the dark Harl could not see much of her face.

'There are more heroes in the world than the people who go up in space ships,' she said.

'I wasn't thinking of her, or of him,' said Harl. 'But the child – think of the danger to the child.'

'We look at things differently,' Ellen said. 'And the child was fine. We used the same radiation on the next two children, and that worked too. All three children are fine, and all of them are telepaths. We are now sure of it.'

'And what happens next?' asked Harl.

'Our generators are already up in space. Five of them can send radiation to everyone in the world.' She laughed. 'That's easy to do these days. Even boring scientists like us can do it.'

'But how can you do a thing like that, after only three experiments?' Harl said. 'Perhaps people don't want it.

9

You haven't asked them, have you? Aren't you afraid that something will go wrong?'

'This is the only way to do it. Think about it. We *have* to change everybody all at the same time. We know how to do it now, and you can't go backwards in science. We can either change everybody at once, or change a few people, here and there, year by year. And if we do that, there will be trouble. How will families with non-telepathic children feel about families with telepathic children? Unhappy, angry, afraid . . . And what happens when people feel like that? They begin fighting to get what they want, and then there'll be war. We don't want that to happen, so we must change everybody in the world now.'

'But after only three experiments,' Harl said again.

'You've forgotten the monkeys. There were five telepathic monkeys in the end, so there were eight experiments, with both monkeys and humans. We can't go on doing experiments for the next fifty or a hundred years. When you want to change the world, you must move quickly. Doing it slowly is very dangerous. We believe that we're doing the right thing, and one day the world will thank us for it.'

'And if I don't agree with you,' said Harl, 'what then? What if I think that you must tell the world about your plan now, while it can still say no?'

'The plan is still secret, and no one will believe you. If

people ask me, I will say that it's all untrue. The other scientists in our group won't talk. So how will you stop it? Where are the generators? Even I don't know that. People will think you are stupid, or crazy. They'll say that you're not the right person to go on a dangerous space journey, and you'll never get to Procyon.'

'Yes,' said HarI. He sounded tired. 'This isn't my world any more. I said goodbye to it when I put my name down for the journey in the *Astronaut*. And if you're right, the world of 2129 will be full of telepaths.' He smiled. 'We can travel back to Procyon if we don't like this world when we get back to it. Or perhaps we'll find nicer people out there, and we'll decide to stay and never come back to Earth.'

'And I shall be dead by then,' said Ellen, 'dead a long time.'

Harl caught her arm quickly. 'Come with us!' he said.

Harl caught Ellen's arm. 'Come with us!' he said.

11

'Then you can see what happens with Project X. Come back and look at your new telepathic world in 2129. Surely you can live eight years in a space ship for that?'

She pulled away from him. 'No. No, Harl. I want to see it now.'

He said: 'Well, if that's what you really want . . .'

They were nearly at the end of the park. In front of them they could see the lights and hear the noise of the city. In the sky above they saw also the sudden white light of the seven o'clock space ship, which was going up from the airport on the far side of the city. In forty-eight hours' time, Harl thought, he would be in one of those ships – flying out into space and leaving the world of 2029 behind for ever. He knew it was true, but sometimes it was hard to believe it. All around him the world was real and unchanging: the noise of traffic, the night's cold wind, the warm, living woman beside him.

He said: 'Tomorrow there will be no time for anything.'

'I know.'

She put her face up to his, and he kissed her.

'I'll leave a letter,' she said, 'for my telepathic great-great-granddaughter. I'll ask her to give you a kiss, for the old days. I'm sure she'll do that for me.'

They were outside the park now. Harl took out his pencil radio and called an airtaxi for Ellen. A second later the airtaxi flew down and came silently to the ground beside them. Harl opened the door and Ellen got in. Then the taxi flew away, and Harl had only the memory of a kiss to carry with him on his long journey.

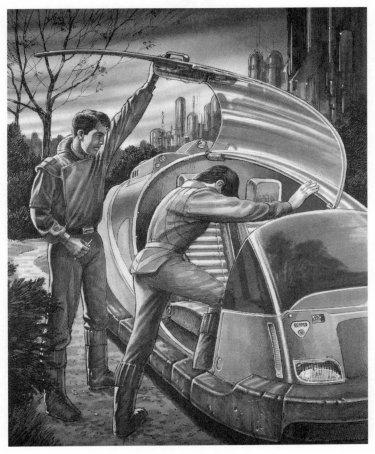

Harl opened the door and Ellen got in.

Chapter 3

2129: Return to Earth

Harl sat with Tom Rennis in the control-room of the *Astronaut.* It was a small room, with not much in it, and Harl knew every corner, every centimetre of it. He could find his way around it with his eyes shut. There was a long, thin crack down one wall, from the crash on Procyon's third planet, more than four years ago.

Harl watched the television screen in front of him and said crossly: 'Can't you get a better picture than that?'

The green thing on the screen was no bigger than a tennis ball. The picture jumped around, went dark, then bright again, and the green thing still looked like a tennis ball. The space ship was still a long way away from Earth.

Rennis was a man who always spoke slowly and carefully. He was still the same after eight long years in the space ship. Sometimes, when the others heard that slow careful voice, they wanted to hit him, but Rennis never got angry. He just went on speaking slowly and carefully.

Now he said: 'Two more days and you won't need to watch Earth on the screen.' He smiled. 'Why don't you use the radio and try to call some of those telepaths down there on Earth.'

When the space ship left Earth eight years before, Harl

14

The green thing still looked like a tennis ball.

told everyone about Project X. He told them how the world would change, how different it would be when they got back. Everyone thought the story was funny, and no one believed him. They laughed at him then, and eight years later they were still laughing at him.

Harl stared at Rennis. 'It doesn't matter to me if people have three heads,' he said. 'They'll be a happy change from the crowd on this ship.'

'The journey's nearly finished,' Rennis said. 'It's been a terrible eight years – I think we all agree about that. None of us knew how hard it would be.'

'You were luckier than most of us,' said Harl. 'You got through it all right, didn't you?'

Rennis smiled lazily. 'True. I'm a slow, silent person, and it's helpful to be like that in difficult times. But it was hard for me too, you know. Shall I tell you what helped me most? I really enjoyed watching all of you when you got angry with me.'

'Sometimes I'd like to break your neck,' said Harl. But he said it without any real anger. For a minute or two he was silent, then he spoke again. 'Tom.'

Rennis looked up from the screen. 'Yes?'

'Those telepaths. I don't want to go through it all again – we've done that so often – but Ellen . . . She is – was – a very clever woman. I believed her. I still do. If she said it was possible to do it, then I believe it *was* possible.'

16

'Weinberg doesn't believe it is,' said Rennis.

'Weinberg didn't believe that the trees on Procyon Two could walk. He believed it only after a tree walked up behind him and nearly took his head off.'

'Yes. I agree that Weinberg is not really the best person to ask. But I have thought about it a bit myself sometimes. In front of the others I've always laughed about it, but, well, I don't know. You're a serious person, Harl; you never tell stupid or untrue stories just to get a laugh. I didn't know Ellen very well, but she was even more serious than you are. So perhaps this story about telepaths *is* true. And if it is, we're going to have a very difficult time.'

'What do you think they will do to us – the non-telepaths?' said Harl.

Rennis smiled again. 'Perhaps they'll put us on a really lonely island in the south Pacific, and tell everybody to stay away from us. That would be the kindest thing to do.'

'Perhaps they'll send us back into space,' said Harl.

'That,' Rennis said, 'is what I'm afraid of.'

When the space ship got nearer the Earth, they tried the radio. They waited to hear the first voices from home, but the radio was silent, and stayed silent.

'Perhaps people don't use radio any more,' said Rennis. 'Perhaps they've got something better now.'

Soon the *Astronaut* was flying round the moon. They

17

watched for the lights of the moon's Tycho City, but the place was dead. On the dark side of the Earth there were no city lights anywhere. The space travellers watched the screens and were silent.

They watched for the lights of the moon's Tycho City, but the place was dead.

The ship came down easily. It hit the wall of air around the Earth and slowed down, circled the world three times, then flew down to its home airfield, just north of Detroit. The date on Earth was the 21st of April, 2129. It was late afternoon, and the sun was shining after rain.

The travellers crowded round the three screens inside the space ship. They stared out into grass which was a metre high. There were trees everywhere on the airfield, young trees, and old trees.

Awkright was now the captain of the *Astronaut* because Lee, the first captain, died on Procyon Two. Awkright turned to the others.

'We'll have to do all the usual checks on air and radiation,' he said quietly. 'If everything's all right, the first group of us will go out in half an hour. While we wait, I'm going to open the last bottle of whisky. I think everyone needs a drink.'

Chapter 4

Where have all the people gone?

Harl stared down at the small glass of whisky in his hand. Rennis, beside him, drank his whisky fast, and held out his glass for some more.

'Well,' Rennis said, 'where are they, Harl? Did these telepaths hear us coming, and decide to fly off to a nicer planet than Earth? If so, they heard us a long way away – while we were still somewhere near Centauri – because there's a tree out there on that airfield which is forty years old, if not more.'

Harl drank his whisky. 'I don't know. Have they – have they just stopped living in cities? Perhaps they don't need cities any more? Cities are dirty, noisy, smelly things.'

'Life,' said Rennis, 'is dirty, noisy, and smelly.'

'Don't be stupid,' Harl said.

'No. What *you* said was stupid. Cities are only a large number of people living together. One way or another, you've got to have them.'

Someone brought in a piece of paper for Awkright. He read it and looked up.

'The air is clean, *very* clean, and there's no radiation. Everything's fine. Mac, Steve, Tom, Peter, Harl – go out

'There's a tree out there on that airfield which is forty years old,
if not more.'

and have a look. Take it easy. We've got a lot of time.'

The men moved to the door of the *Astronaut,* and Steve, the doctor, said: 'Do you think we've gone *back* in time? Perhaps this is the past, not 2129, and America is still full of Indians.'

Harl said: 'Don't forget Tycho City on the moon. There were no lights, but the city was still there.'

And when they got outside, they knew that they were in the future. Across the grass, through the trees, they could see the control-tower. The men began to walk across the airfield, through the tall grass.

The walls of the tower were still standing, but there was nothing inside. It was just an old building, old because of time and weather. There was nothing to tell them why it was empty.

Heavy grey clouds were now hurrying across the sky from the west and it began to rain. The men moved inside the control-tower, and then, without a word, went out again into the rain. They stood with their wet faces turned up to the clouds, remembering what rain was like.

Rennis said: 'This is the worst thing that could happen. The people who said goodbye to us eight years ago are dead – we knew that already. We knew that there would be new people to meet us. But now, there's nobody, just an empty world . . . I don't know how the rest of you feel, but I can feel my dead family all around me.'

They stood with their wet faces turned up to the clouds.

'Yes,' said Harl slowly. *I'll leave a letter for my great-great-granddaughter. I'll ask her to give you a kiss.* Ellen was dead. And there was no great-great-granddaughter to meet him.

'Do you think that people have moved to another part of the world – just stopped living in America?' said Steve.

'Perhaps,' said Rennis. 'But have they also stopped using lights at night? There were no city lights anywhere on the dark side when we flew down to Earth.'

'I don't know,' Steve said. He pushed his hand through his hair, and rain ran down his face. 'I just don't know.'

'Come on,' Harl said. 'We'll walk on into Detroit.'

23

In the city there were fewer trees, and grass grew only in places, in the cracks in the streets. Most of the buildings were still standing, but they were silent and empty. The men walked on into the city centre, and then turned and walked back to the space ship. It was getting dark by the time they got there.

The buildings were silent and empty.

24

Awkright said: 'Well? Nothing?'

'Nothing,' Harl told him. 'There's no one there. I'm sure of it. We went a bit crazy for a while – shouted and screamed and sang songs very loudly. Nothing happened and nobody came. There wasn't anybody to come.'

'I didn't think there would be,' Awkright said.

'Can you explain it?'

'No.'

'So what do we do?'

'Tomorrow we'll put a balloon up,' said Awkright. 'If there's a group of people somewhere near here, they'll see it and perhaps come to find out what it is. We'll put a light on it at night. And you can take the *Astronaut's* little space car, and fly round the rest of the planet. Don't spend a lot of time looking at cities, but give the bigger ones a quick look over. Take three or four days to do it. Now we'll get a night's sleep; in good, clean air.'

Chapter 5

A look around the Earth

A few days later Harl and Rennis flew the space car back down to the airfield. When they got out, they saw that the long grass was now much shorter. Some of the others were still busy cutting it near the control-tower. High above them in the sky, at a thousand metres, a big balloon turned slowly in the wind, first this way, then that way.

Awkright came out to meet them.

'I can see from your unhappy faces,' he said, 'that you haven't found anything. And nothing's come in to us. Come and have dinner. You can talk while we eat.'

The bottom room of the control-tower was now a living-room. It looked cleaner and tidier than before, and smelled better too.

'We eat in here,' said Awkright, 'but we still sleep in the *Astronaut*. We don't want to move until we know what we are going to do next. How was New York?'

'Dead,' Harl said. 'We saw a whale in the river under Brooklyn Bridge – well, the part of the bridge that was still standing.'

'And Paris . . . London . . . Rome?'

'Like Baghdad, Delhi, and Tokyo – all dead. We saw

High in the sky, a big balloon turned slowly in the wind.

lions in the streets in Rome. They were hunting wild pigs.
Tell him about that, Tom.'

'It was interesting,' Rennis said. 'We were flying very
slowly, at about twenty metres above the ground. There's
a big road which goes from the Coliseum to a large square.

27

A lion was going along this road behind two wild pigs – it wasn't trying to catch them, it was just moving them along. They tried to run off down a side street, but a second lion was waiting at the corner and stopped them going that way. When the pigs tried to break out on the other side, there was a third lion there. The fourth lion was waiting for them in the square.'

'The fourth lion was waiting for them in the square.'

'So?' Awkright said.

'Think about it,' said Harl. 'Remember what the world is like now. Humans know what another person is feeling, seeing, hearing, smelling. They don't have to think about it; they just *know*. And all living things – humans *and* animals – are the same. So what happens to your wild animals, which hunt for their food?'

Awkright thought about it. 'They don't catch anything,' he said slowly. 'The pig knows when the lion is coming up behind it. If a cat tries to catch a bird, the bird will always fly away before the cat can jump on it.'

'That's right,' said Harl. 'The animals that can run fast and can have a lot of babies quickly will be fine. The animals that eat grass and leaves will be all right, but the ones that eat meat will have a difficult time. But there's an answer to it. The lions had it. Animals that hunt have learned to work together. So life goes on as before: the pig can't easily escape from a group of lions working together.'

Awkright shook his head unhappily. 'This is terrible!' he said. 'You told us about the first experiments with monkeys. Does this mean that those generators of Project X changed everything on the planet? Everything living?'

'Not everything living, perhaps,' said Harl. 'Some of the very small animals and fish don't really think – they haven't really got minds. You have to have something to

29

think *with* before you can be telepathic. But I can't tell you which animals are telepathic and which aren't.'

'And does this explain why the world is empty of people?'

'No,' Harl said slowly. 'I don't see how it can explain that. But there isn't any other way to explain it, is there?'

'Isn't there?' Rennis asked. 'Two strange things happen. First, all humans and animals change into telepaths. Second, we come back to find a world empty of humans. We put the two things together, of course, because when you have an x and a y, you always try to make them into an equation, just like $3\times4=2\times6$. But perhaps the two things just don't go together. x is telepathy, and y is a world empty of humans. Two different, unknown things. No equation.'

'But why is the world empty of humans?' said Harl. 'The only answer to that question is telepathy. You can't give me any other answers, can you? Come on, give me one now.'

'Give me your equation which shows that x and y go together.'

Harl shook his head. 'I don't know,' he said. 'We just don't understand any of it.'

'When we were on the *Astronaut*,' Awkright said, 'I was always laughing at you, Harl. Oh, those wonderful telepaths back on Earth! When we got home, you said, they would put us strange old humans in a zoo, with all the other wild animals. Well, I would like to be in a zoo right now, I really would. I'd like to sit there in my cage and

'I would like to be in a zoo right now, I really would.'

watch the children, while they walked past us, eating chocolate, staring at us, talking and laughing. I'd stand on my head for them. Happily.'

31

Chapter 6

News from an old man

Harl was standing near the *Astronaut* the next morning, when the visitor arrived. Harl watched the man carefully. At first he couldn't believe his eyes. He was afraid that he was seeing another walking tree or something, so he didn't call the others. But it was a man; strange-looking, but a real living man. He was very, very old. His clothes were old and dirty, and he was riding a thin, tired horse. He rode up to Harl, and got shakily down to stand beside him. He was crying and smiling at the same time.

'I did it,' he said. 'I said I'd stay alive until you came back, and I have. Years ago, I lived here, near the airfield, but the wild animals moved away, and I had to follow them. They travel around in strange ways now.'

'How old are you?' Harl asked.

He thought immediately what a strange question it was. Here, suddenly, was a human in front of him – perhaps the last one still alive. Harl turned his head to the control-tower and shouted:

'Look who's come!'

The old man said: 'I think I'm nearly a hundred years old.' He smiled. 'I was born in the same year that the

32

It was a man; strange-looking, but a real living man.

Astronaut left Earth. They called me Lee, the same name as your space ship's captain had.'

'He's dead,' Harl said.

Tom Rennis and Steve were hurrying up to them, with Awkright just behind them.

'I'm sorry about that,' said the old man. 'Did many of you die?'

'Only one,' said Harl.

Awkright arrived and said: 'Well, where are they?'

'I haven't asked him yet,' said Harl.

'The people?' the old man said. 'You mean the rest of the people? They died. I had two friends with me until the hard winter, the year before last. That killed them. You get lonely by yourself. I wasn't sure that I could remember how to talk. I never did like talking to myself.'

Harl said: 'Hey! He was born in the year that the *Astronaut* went out – before the generators started. Does that mean . . . there was something wrong? The radiation didn't make telepaths, just killed everybody? But the animals today! And Whittaker's children . . .'

'You knew about the generators, then?' the old man said.

He smiled at them happily. It was not surprising that he was a bit crazy. He was a very old man, near the end of a long hard life. But the others were in a hurry to get his news out of him. Awkright took hold of his arm.

34

'Look,' he said, 'what did the generators do?'

'They made telepaths. You didn't know that? All the children were telepaths – and the animals, too. It's difficult to catch the animals because you can't get near them. But the telepathy only works up to about half a kilometre away, so you're all right if you've got a special hunting gun which can shoot a long way. I've got a gun like that, but my eyes aren't so good these last years.'

'You're all right if you've got a special gun which can shoot a long way.'

35

Awkright said, slowly and carefully, 'What happened to the telepaths?'

'Some of them grew to be adults,' the old man said. 'But not many. They were all right when they were young children, most of them. But when they were about ten or

'They could see, hear, feel everything, every minute of their waking lives.'

eleven years old, they began to die like flies, one after the other. Perhaps one in a hundred grew to be twenty. I had two children myself. People were always hoping that the telepathy would stop one day, but the scientists said it would never stop. My boy got to fifteen.'

'But why did they die?' Rennis asked him. 'What killed them? Were they ill in some way?'

The old man looked at him in surprise. 'Why, no,' he said. 'The telepathy killed them, of course.' To him, there was no question about it. He didn't understand the need to explain it. 'That was the only thing that killed them. Some of them shot themselves or jumped off buildings, things like that, but most of them just died.'

'But why?' Harl said. 'Why?'

'Because people have got bad minds. That's why. Look at yourself deep down inside. You know what you're really like, don't you? Not very nice, mostly, and it's not comfortable to think about it, is it? So we don't. We hide from our true selves, and when we speak, we don't always say what we think or feel. So we hide from other people too, and they hide from us. But the telepaths couldn't escape, could they? They knew all the terrible things that went on in their minds, and they knew what went on in other people's minds too. They could see, hear, feel everything, every minute of their waking lives. Think about it – living with that terrible noise of other people's

37

minds in your head all the time. So, when the children got to about ten years old, it hit them and it went on hitting them. If a child was a nice, kind person, the telepathy killed him more quickly – or her, but the girls lived longer, mostly.'

Awkright turned his head away. 'So that's how it was,' he said. He sounded tired.

'But didn't some people change . . . learn to live with it?' asked Rennis. 'Perhaps there are still some telepaths living somewhere in the world – with their children . . .?'

'Their children?' The old man laughed. 'The older telepaths never married and never had children. It was bad just living with yourself. And how can you love someone when all the time you can see deep down into their mind?'

It was a bright spring morning. There was white blossom on one of the trees beside them, and a soft warm wind played with the flowers.

'After thousands of years,' Awkright said, 'it comes to this.'

The old man said: 'That's why I wanted to live until you came back. I wanted to see things start again.'

They looked at him.

'They called me Lee after the captain,' he said again. 'I knew all about the *Astronaut's* journey. I read all the papers. I knew that there were two women on the space ship. Things can start again now.'

Rennis and Awkright turned and began to walk away.

'Yes,' Harl said. 'Two women. Mary Rogers and Lucy Parino. Mary is fifty-two years old and Lucy is fifty-four.'

On the tree beside them the white blossom, bright in the spring sunshine, danced in the warm wind.

GLOSSARY

astronaut a space traveller; (in this story) the name of the space ship

balloon a very large strong bag filled with hot air, which goes up into the sky

believe to think that something is true

blossom all the flowers on a tree

cage a box or a place with bars round it for keeping animals or birds

captain the leader of a group of people

check (*v*) to look to see if something is all right

city a large town

clean (*adj*) not dirty

control (room/tower) a room or tall building where people tell aeroplanes, space ships, etc., what to do

crack (*n*) a long, very thin and narrow hole in something

crazy mad, strange in the head

earth the planet that we live on

equation a way of saying (in mathematics) that two things are equal, e.g. 7x4=30-2

experiment something that people do to find out and study what happens

generator a machine that makes electricity

grass a plant with thin green leaves that cows eat

great-great-granddaughter the granddaughter of your grandchild

grow to get bigger, taller, longer, older, etc.

hero a very brave person

human a person

hunt to chase and kill animals for food
kiss to touch someone with your lips in a loving way
lion a large, yellow-brown, dangerous kind of wild cat
memory something that you remember
mind (*n*) the part of the head that thinks, feels, and remembers
monkey an animal with a long tail that lives in trees, and is most like a human
park a large garden, often in a town, for people to walk or play in
pig a fat (often pink or white) farm animal
planet a 'world' in the sky that moves round a sun
project a big plan of work
radiation the sending out of heat and other things that you can't see (e.g. radiation from the sun can burn the skin)
science the study of natural things, e.g. physics, biology
scientist a person who studies one of the sciences
serious not funny or playful
space ship a ship that can travel through space to planets and stars
stare (*v*) to look hard at something for a long time
telepath a person who knows what other people are thinking and feeling, without the use of words
telepathic of or using telepathy
telepathy sending and receiving thoughts and feelings from one mind to another, without the use of words
war fighting between countries, or between large groups of people in one country
whale the biggest sea-animal
whisky a strong alcoholic drink
zoo a place where many different kinds of wild animals are kept for people to look at

Return to Earth

ACTIVITIES

Before Reading

1 **Read the back cover and the story introduction on the first page of the book. How much do you know now about the story? Tick one box for each sentence.**

	YES	NO
1 Harl plans to travel to the moon.	☐	☐
2 Ellen and Harl work in a park.	☐	☐
3 Ellen wants to stay on Earth.	☐	☐
4 Love comes first for Harl and Ellen.	☐	☐
5 Ellen is a scientist.	☐	☐
6 Ellen listens to the radio all the time.	☐	☐
7 Harl's journey into space will be for several weeks.	☐	☐
8 Harl's journey will be dangerous.	☐	☐

2 **What is going to happen in this story? Choose Y (yes) or N (no) for each ending to this sentence.**

When Harl returns to Earth, . . .
1 he will marry Ellen. Y/N
2 Ellen will be dead. Y/N
3 the human mind will be different. Y/N
4 he will be a very old man. Y/N

3 **This story ends in the year 2129. What do *you* think the world will be like then?**
Tick one box for each sentence.

	YES	NO	PERHAPS
1 People will live longer.	☐	☐	☐
2 People will be happier.	☐	☐	☐
3 People will have more free time.	☐	☐	☐
4 People will travel to the moon.	☐	☐	☐
5 There will be no fighting between countries.	☐	☐	☐
6 Cities will be cleaner, and nicer.	☐	☐	☐
7 Computers will do all the boring jobs.	☐	☐	☐
8 People will never be ill, unhappy or bored.	☐	☐	☐

4 **Is telepathy possible? Can *you* 'hear' other people's thoughts in their minds? Which of these sentences about telepathy do you agree with?**

1 It is possible, but I have never done it.
2 It is possible, and I know somebody who has done it.
3 It is possible, but it doesn't happen very often.
4 It happens a lot, but people don't usually notice it.
5 People think it happens, but it's just luck.
6 Perhaps we will learn to do it one day.
7 It just isn't possible.

While Reading

Read Chapters 1 and 2. Whose ideas are these – Harl's or Ellen's?

1 Living on a space ship will be terrible.
2 The world will be a very different place by 2129.
3 The *Astronaut* project is more important than Project X.
4 Arthur Whittaker and his wife are heroes.
5 Changing the world slowly is dangerous.
6 Perhaps people won't want to be telepaths.
7 The scientists must tell people about Project X before it happens.
8 It is not possible to stop Project X.

Read Chapter 3, then circle the correct words in each sentence.

1 The space travellers were *eight/a hundred* years older.
2 On Earth it was *eight/a hundred* years later.
3 The journey on the space ship was very *difficult/easy*.
4 The space travellers were *worried/happy* about a world full of telepaths.
5 When they tried the radio, they heard *voices/nothing*.
6 On Detroit airfield there were *planes/trees* everywhere.

Before you read Chapter 4, can you guess what happened on Earth? Which answer do you prefer?

1 After Project X, there was a terrible war and many people died. Only a few people are alive on Earth now.
2 Project X killed everybody.
3 The world is now full of telepaths, who live beautiful, easy lives. Everybody is happy and nobody ever fights.
4 Telepaths are very unhappy people.
5 Project X changed the human mind in many ways. People now live like wild animals and fight all the time.

Read Chapters 4 and 5. Here are some untrue sentences about them. Change them into true sentences.

1 The air on Earth was very dirty.
2 The travellers knew that they were in the past.
3 The travellers saw some children in Detroit.
4 Paris, London and Tokyo were all busy.
5 Project X didn't change any animals.
6 The travellers understood why there were no humans.

Before you read Chapter 6 (the title is *News from an old man*), can you guess the answers to these questions?

1 How old is the old man?
2 What is his news?

After Reading

1 **After the old man arrived, Captain Awkright wrote his diary for that day. Join these halves of sentences together to make a paragraph of seven sentences.**

1 Today an old man came to the airfield, . . .
2 He told us all about Project X, and . . .
3 When most of the children were about ten or eleven, . . .
4 The older ones never married . . .
5 The old man waited for us, full of hope, because . . .
6 Here on Earth it is spring, . . .
7 Mary and Lucy are too old to have children, . . .
8 but there is no new life for us.
9 they either died or killed themselves.
10 but he brought some terrible news.
11 he knew that there were two women on our space ship.
12 so we will be the last people on Earth.
13 what happened to the telepaths.
14 and never had children.

2 **Find the answers to this crossword in the story.**

1 Drewitt used this in his experiments on unborn monkeys. (9)
2 A machine that makes electricity. (9)

3 Awkright put one of these into the sky above the control tower. (7)

4 The scientists did eight _____ with monkeys and humans. (11)

5 Ellen and Drewitt worked on _____ X. (7)

6 Harl's space ship was called the _____. (9)

7 Harl, Ellen and Drewitt were _____. (10)

8 Harl wanted to go on his dangerous journey and be a _____ of space travel. (4)

9 Drewitt used this animal in his experiments. (6)

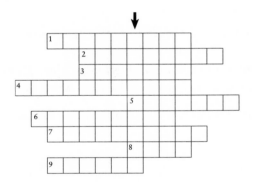

What is the word in the crossword below the arrow? Choose and tick the best clue for this word.

1 Remembering things.

2 Studying the minds of humans and animals.

3 Sending thoughts from one person to another.

3 **People in the story said these things about the future. Were they right or wrong? Explain why.**

In 2029:

1 HARL: 'When I get back, I'll say hello to your great-great-granddaughter.'

2 ELLEN: 'There will be no wives for you in the world of 2129.'

3 ELLEN: 'One day the world will thank us for telepathy.'

In 2129:

4 RENNIS: 'Perhaps they will put us on a really lonely island in the south Pacific.'

5 LEE (the old man): 'Things can start again now.'

4 **Perhaps Ellen wrote a letter and left it for Harl. Complete it with the linking words below. (Use each word once.)**

now / perhaps / if / at first / so / and / who / because / when / then

Detroit, 13th August 2045

Dear Harl,

_____ you will read this letter one day. I wanted to write it to tell you about Project X. _____ everybody was really happy and excited about it, _____ Drewitt and Whittaker became famous all over the world.

_____, after a few years, the children started to die. _____ they were about ten, the telepathy killed them. I had

50

two daughters _____ were telepathic. _____ they are both dead, _____ I don't want to live any longer.

_____ you can find a better world, Harl, please go there. Remember me sometimes, _____ I have always remembered our last day in the park, and your last kiss.
Goodbye,
Ellen

5 **Which of these ideas do you agree (A) or disagree (D) with?**

1 It is wrong to try to change the human mind.
2 Scientists must try new things all the time. If they don't do that, we will never learn anything new.
3 Space travel is very expensive, and it isn't necessary. We need the money for other things.
4 Space travel is important. Perhaps there is life on other planets, and we must find it.

6 **Here are some other titles for this story. Which are good (G) and which are not good (NG)? Can you explain why?**

Project X   The Last Humans
Journey to Procyon   Living With Telepathy
Starting Again   Harl and Ellen
An Empty Future   A Dangerous Science

ABOUT THE AUTHOR

John Christopher (1922–), has been writing fiction for fifty years. He has five children and many grandchildren, and lives in Sussex, in the south of England. He has written for both adults and children, and many of his books are described as science fiction.

Those books are often about a world after something strange and terrible has happened. What do people do when this happens? How do they learn to live in a world that has changed so much? Does science make people's lives happier, or not? John Christopher's books explore questions like these.

Among his books, the Tripods trilogy (*The White Mountains*, *The City of Gold and Lead*, *The Pool of Fire*) is the most popular with children. It is in print all over the world, including Iran (where it is the most popular English book for young adults). *The Death of Grass* is his best-known adult title. John Christopher's own favourites are the books in his *Sword of the Spirits* trilogy.

ABOUT BOOKWORMS

OXFORD BOOKWORMS LIBRARY
Classics • True Stories • Fantasy & Horror • Human Interest
Crime & Mystery • Thriller & Adventure

The OXFORD BOOKWORMS LIBRARY offers a wide range of original and adapted stories, both classic and modern, which take learners from elementary to advanced level through six carefully graded language stages:

Stage 1 (400 headwords)	**Stage 4** (1400 headwords)
Stage 2 (700 headwords)	**Stage 5** (1800 headwords)
Stage 3 (1000 headwords)	**Stage 6** (2500 headwords)

More than fifty titles are also available on cassette, and there are many titles at Stages 1 to 4 which are specially recommended for younger learners. In addition to the introductions and activities in each Bookworm, resource material includes photocopiable test worksheets and Teacher's Handbooks, which contain advice on running a class library and using cassettes, and the answers for the activities in the books.

Several other series are linked to the OXFORD BOOKWORMS LIBRARY. They range from highly illustrated readers for young learners, to playscripts, non-fiction readers, and unsimplified texts for advanced learners.

Oxford Bookworms Starters	*Oxford Bookworms Factfiles*
Oxford Bookworms Playscripts	*Oxford Bookworms Collection*

Details of these series and a full list of all titles in the OXFORD BOOKWORMS LIBRARY can be found in the *Oxford English* catalogues. A selection of titles from the OXFORD BOOKWORMS LIBRARY can be found on the next pages.

BOOKWORMS · FANTASY & HORROR · STAGE 2

The Year of Sharing

HARRY GILBERT

Richard is bored with the quiet life of his village. He would like to have a motor-car and drive it . . . very fast. But Richard lives in a future world where there are no cars, only bicycles and small villages and green forests.

And now he is twelve years old, and like the other children, he must do his Year of Sharing. He must live alone in the forest with the wild animals. He must learn to share his world; he must learn how animals live and eat and fight . . . and die.

BOOKWORMS · CRIME & MYSTERY · STAGE 2

Death in the Freezer

TIM VICARY

Ellen Shore's family is an ordinary American family, and Ellen is six years old when her brother Al is born. Her parents are very pleased to have a son, but Ellen is not pleased, because now baby Al comes first.

And when they are adults, Al still comes first. He begins a rock band and makes records. Soon he is rich and famous – very rich, but he gives nothing to his sister Ellen. She has a difficult life, with three young kids and very little money. And she learns to hate her rich, famous, unkind brother . . .

Voodoo Island

MICHAEL DUCKWORTH

Mr James Conway wants to make money. He wants to build new houses and shops – and he wants to build them on an old graveyard, on the island of Haiti.

There is only one old man who still visits the graveyard; and Mr Conway is not afraid of one old man.

But the old man has friends – friends in the graveyard, friends who lie dead, under the ground. And when Mr Conway starts to build his houses, he makes the terrible mistake of disturbing the sleep of the dead . . .

Dracula

BRAM STOKER

Retold by Diane Mowat

In the mountains of Transylvania there stands a castle. It is the home of Count Dracula – a dark, lonely place, and at night the wolves howl around the walls.

In the year 1875 Jonathan Harker comes from England to do business with the Count. But Jonathan does not feel comfortable at Castle Dracula. Strange things happen at night, and very soon, he begins to feel afraid. And he is right to be afraid, because Count Dracula is one of the Un-Dead – a vampire that drinks the blood of living people . . .

The Mystery of Allegra

PETER FOREMAN

Allegra is an unusual name. It means 'happy' in Italian, but the little girl in this story is sometimes very sad. She is only five years old, but she tells Adrian, her new friend, that she is going to die soon. How does she know?

And who is the other Allegra? The girl in a long white nightdress, who has golden hair and big blue eyes. The girl who comes only at night, and whose hands and face are cold, so cold . . .

The Star Zoo

HARRY GILBERT

In our world today a hummingbird is a small, brilliantly coloured bird that lives in the tall trees of tropical forests.

In the far distant future, Hummingbird (Hummy for short) is a girl of sixteen who lives somewhere in the Galaxy, on a planet called Just Like Home. She has the name 'Hummingbird' in big letters on all her clothes, but she has never seen a real hummingbird. She has never seen any living animal or bird at all. The Book of Remembering says that there were once many animals on a planet called Earth, but that was before the Burning, a long, long time ago . . .